The Break Up Tapes
by Jacqueline Gallegos

© 2025 Jacqueline Gallegos
All rights reserved.

No part of this book may be reproduced, stored in a retrieval system, or transmitted in any form or by any means—electronic, mechanical, photocopying, recording, or otherwise—without the prior written permission of the author, except for brief quotations used in reviews or scholarly works.

Published by: Rawmeash

ISBN: 978-0-9913547-6-4

First Edition

For *The Unnameables*, without whom this book would not be possible. It's been nearly 7 years writing together. My work has grown immensely thanks to your careful eyes, critique, and friendship.

And for Edgar, my husband. You love me in the way I have been seeking. Thank you for encouraging me to always keep finding myself. Me importas tú y nadie más que tú.

"The heart of another is a dark forest, always, no matter how close it has been to one's own."

- Willa Cather

THE BREAK UP TAPES

PART I

In Love With Possibility 17

Moonlight Cheeks 18

We Could Be Something Special 19

Tend 21

No One But You 22

You Ask Me How I Know I Love You 23

Love Is Worry 24

PART II

Sunset I'm Outrunning 29

Stay With Me 30

Misfit 32

What Do You Want Me To Call You? 33

Two Minutes 35

Buttercup 37

Paper Thin 39

Sad Dog 40

To Go 41

I'm Okay 42

Eye of The Storm 44

It Didn't Hurt Until It Did or Don't Ask Questions You Don't Want The Answer To 45

Recipe To Mend A Broken Heart 46

PART III

Don't Feel Bad At All 51

(Why Unsending DMs Is A God Send In Your) Hoe Phase 52

Flaming Dog Shit 56

I Should "Allow" Men To Date Me 58

Rattled 60

God Bless 62

Balloons 63

Photo Gallery 66

Thank You 71

Acknowledgements 73

About The Author 75

Part I

In Love With Possibility

You are the most beautiful person I've never seen
Your laugh full and surprising
Eyes squinting and tearing up
Expressions that won't let you keep anything to yourself
Hold my hand like a promise

Maybe we've already met
As friends of friends
Or passing by on a crowded sidewalk
Sweeping hair out of my face when we lock eyes
You look back at me
 Do I know you?

Either way, I'll keep my window open at night
Sleep only on one side
So there's just enough room for you

And you'll find me
Drift through the cold air
Brush my face to wake me

Others have said
I love you
But talk is cheap
A wishing well, they throw pennies at my feet

They could never gaze at an unremarkable sky with me
And understand how the vastness swallows me speechless

You would know when to just be with me
When my body wants to be held
Tell me what I don't want to hear, but need to
And listen to the childhood stories I don't tell people

Moonlight Cheeks

When I see you again
After all this time
It's in a black bowler hat and mustache
Outlined in a funnel of pale, warm light

The walls melt away
We're standing in the open-air night

All there is
Or will be
Are moonlight cheeks

And the years—
They're reflecting in your eyes
Rewinding and pausing at
The highlight reels

I forget myself
I could believe we were in the 1920s
Or some other lost decade
If you caressed me once

We Could Be Something Special

Daylight came to die in your room
You're face down in bed with a lilac sheet covering your waist
We share a pillow
My hand peaking and dipping over your shoulder blades and spine
Hearing it in my head
"We could be something special"
"We have something special"
I practiced it in the car

Minutes go by
We switch positions
The silence is comfortable
Almost feel bad breaking it
I hear it in my head again
Hate the idea of pillow talk
Like I wouldn't say it in the kitchen or on the couch
Like I only feel this here and now because I'm soft

Your hand is on my hair
Not stroking it, just still
Half asleep
Looking at your chest while lying on you
I say
You know...we have something special
You answer
Mhmm
I watch the dust dance in the last streaks of sun
Wonder if there's a name for that
You open your eyes
What do you mean?
I lift my chin toward you and exhale
    I like spending time with you
    I feel comfortable with you
    I like you
It comes out too fast and nothing like I'd pictured

You're quiet

My pulse a stopwatch
You close your eyes
And start stroking my hair

TEND

I want to be the secret you can't keep
My name slipping into all your stories
Your friends begging to see my photo
When you think of me
A smile so big your cheeks hurt

I want you to tend the flame
Let it be just as warm years from now

Don't want to stop at a spark
        (I cannot be called a "flash in the pan" again)
Or fizzle out to an old flame
        (Are you the one who will stay?)
Let me be the heat in your chest
        (Flirt with me forever)
That stokes you awake
        (The reason you get up today)

No One But You

Me importas tú y tú y tú y solamente tú y tú y tú
Me importas tú y tú y tú y nadie más que tú

My love played this song for me
Told me his grandfather Antonio
Was a famous steel string guitarist in Mexico
Sat outside his family store when the sun slept
Him and his friends singing to the stars

Antonio said once a young man and his girlfriend walked by late at night, fighting
The men played a serenade just for her
The couple walked away holding hands

I listen to the lyrics, let the plucky beat soothe my breathing,
Make me feel like I'm in an old movie and everything is easy
Wonder why life can't be that sweet and simple

Maybe it can
Me importas tú
    You matter to me
Nadie más que tú
    No one but you

You Ask Me How I Know I Love You

We went to Europe for two weeks
Just you and I
Drinking 1 euro espressos at each corner
And I never wanted space

If I could, I would mainline you
Let you tingle through me

If we were in The States, I'd turn you into a Big Gulp
Suck you down and pay 1 dollar for a refill over and over

And the 40 years we might get
They're cheapened with obligation
Work mostly, physical therapy for my bum knee,
Appointments with a doctor telling me how to slow death,
All of it amounting to less time drinking you down

I want hours in the stolen night
Telling you all the funny things I thought of
When you were away

I want you to be there for it all

LOVE IS WORRY

Love is seasick butterflies
Surging up my throat
When you fall asleep before
Texting that you made it
Home safely

Part II

Sunset I'm Outrunning

I want to drive fast with the music loud and the windows down
The wind to blow hair around my face like a halo
Like our life is a movie I'd pay to see

I want the sunlight to hit your eyes just right
To glint like there's nowhere else you'd rather be
Your smile to seem like it's for my eyes only

The perfect song would come on
We'd sing and scream
Your voice in just the right key
I can't sing
But at least I'd know the words

I want to keep us frozen here
In a moving picture I can frame on my shelf
To live in our movie
And never have to hear the words I know are coming
The sunset I'm outrunning

Stay With Me

We're circling around in a shuffle waltz
Your hands on my hips
My head finds the smooth dip in your shoulder
Rests there with eyes closed against the haze

You haven't touched me in months
But now, here we are
Slow dancing in our 1 bedroom apartment

We rented this place months ago
(But I've been paying your rent)
You never wanted to hang art
Didn't come the day my family drove around town
For our secondhand furniture

Remember that Sunday I waited for you?
Our waffles getting cold
Your voicemail full
When you came home, I was on the couch in the dark
Puffy eyes and my body tight
You had nothing to say except hello

I tried to tell you with my eyes I love you
Your mouth told me I care about you

Now here we are
Our apartment slowly being enveloped in flames
Fire licking my feet
Burning the rubber soles of my shoes
But I don't feel it

Watching little ash snowflakes dance around us
Holding each other while the smoke sears our lungs
Rocking back and forth in the glow
And it is warm
So warm

I want to tell you all the things my eyes tried to say

The words grip the insides of my mouth, refuse to come out
So I just sway

Misfit

Yellow traffic lights that turn red too fast
A noisy restaurant and "I didn't quite catch that"
A pair of jeans a little too tight
The song where I never get the words right

My left shoe is two inches too tall
And I'm walking all wrong
I hold your hand, hide my limp
Walk into the tomorrow you promised us

I keep breezing through the yellowreds
Laughing and nodding like I heard what you said
Suck my gut in and pull us on like pants that barely zip
Gasping, I mouth the words you want to hear

WHAT DO YOU WANT ME TO CALL YOU?

You moved into a new apartment
One bedroom all by yourself
I bought you a microwave
Wrote a tardy Valentine
A cheesy line about our romance *heating up*
You tilt your head, eyes twinkling in the early afternoon sun
    "That's cute, boo" and add:
    "I'm sorry I didn't get you anything"
I flash you an *it's-okay-baby*-smile

We crack the champagne I brought
Drink mimosas from glasses
Meant for another type of drink
Unpack your house
I'm careful with your things, like they were my own

I've gathered all the orphaned boxes
Ask you to recycle them with me

We run into your landlord outside
You two exchange names and then he gestures towards me
    You say: "Oh this is my friend.
    She's helping me move in."
I give a nod as my hands are filled with boxes
Walk behind the cinderblock wall
Hear your landlord jest that you 'needed a woman's touch' and you laughing
I imagine him slapping your back with a *that-a-boy* rhythm
And you shooting him a *you're-goddamn-right*-smile

You come join me at the dumpster
I turn to you in a hushed tone,
    "I'm your friend, huh?"
You're crushing the seam of a box underfoot
Eyes on the cardboard as you tease,
    "What do you want me to call you?"

I make a joke about older people not understanding

How millennials date
We agree
We don't know what to call each other

For months, we float like this
Our little boat propelled on the crests and dips
A captain-less vessel heading for a promise
In a sea full of nothing

On a warm summer Thursday, I text you to check in
About our plans for this weekend
You say you hurt your shoulder
And we may need to cancel

I write, "It's okay. I'm kind of in a funk anyway"
    You reply, "Do you know what caused it?
    Sometimes it just happens to me randomly :/ "
I send some answer that isn't vague enough
In ten seconds my phone rings, your name on my screen

We break up,
Split,
Jump ship,
Or whatever it is you call this
You thank me
    "for always being so communicative, Jacqueline"
I mutter a mirror of that back
Call you brave for telling me how you feel
But never call you your name

Two Minutes

One line is good. Two lines are bad. I have to wait between two-ten minutes to read the results. After ten, the results are no good and I'll have to throw the test out. That's why I bought three– the pricey ones. This isn't something you cheap out on. Really need to be sure about those faint, barely there blue lines. Why call yourself *Clear Blue* when it's not very clear or very blue? I put the box back down on the table. I start pacing around in my small kitchen, pressing the peeling, bumpy linoleum down with my toes like a giant roll of bubble wrap.

Last time I did this, I was so nervous. That was in high school. Thinking my parents would find out, I hid the box in a neighbor's bush. Was too panicky to throw it in the trash. In retrospect, that was dumb. I could've just brought it to school and thrown it out there. Back then the lines were pink and the test was from Dollar Tree because no one's Mom or Auntie I knew worked there. Still had to buy three anyway just to be sure.

I'm still pacing. Probably looking like an epileptic rooster. Good thing I live alone. God has it been two minutes yet? I recently learned they call pregnancies past 36 "geriatric." Like they need a gurney, or a cup of Jell-O and some BINGO. It makes my 28 feel too close to expiration. Is this the pressure Olympians feel? Once you age out of your prime, what are you to the world besides a photo of you in your heyday on the cover of a *Women's Health* magazine?

I was an egg donor. It's how I paid for grad school to become a teacher. The doctors said I was twice as fertile as women my age, so they took that many eggs. Never thought I'd need them. Or want them. Do I?

The other night, I was selling Water Polo tickets at the high school. I was teamed up with a leadership student. I think her name was Noah. She had her notebook out and was doodling on her unfinished Math homework.
Without looking up she asked, "do you have kids?"
I laughed, "I'm 28. I'm still young. Maybe someday."

Like 28 isn't close to 30. And 30 is when everyone expects you to have: a husband, and 2.5 kids, a dog, a house. What's with the .5? Is King Solomon going to come down from the heavens and offer me half a child to test my wisdom? Noah's making change for a family here to see the game. She looks over at me and smiles, returning to her doodling. I hope Noah's never had to hide a box in the bushes.

My phone alarm goes off. Finally. One line. That says one line. On three different tests.

Buttercup

Being the poor thing waiting by the phone all night for your Buttercup / Pretending you're cool and relaxed but instead you're waiting for the edge of a word from that certain someone / Only half breathing in fear that you won't be able to hear the phone / And when the sleep starts overtaking you / When "I told you so" forms on your lips / You feel ridiculous / Like you've been wronged but saw it coming miles away / I mean yes, you were just sitting here reading / Half falling asleep on the couch and waiting for word / For plans made and now maybe misplaced / Want to believe they just lost track of time / They meant to call /

You'll give them 20 more minutes / I mean, it is a Sunday / Can't well be up all night here / Get up to flip the record over / There's something comforting in listening to sappy, old love music / It's like crying in the rain without having to go outside / And their heartache makes you feel like love only hurts if you're doing it right /

When those extra 20 minutes come and go / The line in the sand you keep erasing and redrawing / You decide you have too much pride to call first / (Like last time) / Expect some kind of apology tomorrow / Will have to compose yourself into "it's okays!" / Lilt your voice into a toothy smile / Can't come off too disappointed / Can't let them know you hardly used the bathroom in fear you may miss the call /

And you start singing along mindlessly / Not noticing you're carrying the world's lost loves on your lips / Like you're in the middle of an oldies song in the making / You remember this Amy Winehouse interview where she laments how old love music was tragically beautiful / You declared your love and how you would just lay down, rip out your heart to show it to them, and die in the road / Music now, she said, is all about how we don't need anyone else. / How no one really knows us. / We've already moved on. /

I want to wait for my Buttercup by the phone / But only if I can tell you I practically laid down and died in the silence / Only we live now / And I know it would scare you away / So I sit here convincing myself tomorrow's apology must be real good / Or that I have to decide if I'm okay with the more likely scenario / That you don't mention it at all. /

Paper Thin

Steady
      bump di bump bump
      bump di bump bump
      bump di bump bump
Vibrating through the other side of our apartment wall

Neighbor always playing something past quiet hours
      I think I heard them moaning
Over the Top 40's hits I hate, but can sing along to

Makes me wish he would touch me

The last day we had sex
Was when we moved in
Three months ago

And I hear the
      bump di bump bump
      bump di bump bump
      bump di bump bump
Through our thin walls
And wish it was us making loud love

Sad Dog

The only reason to go to sleep
Is so I don't have to think

The internet is making me dumber and sadder and terrible
Browse your life without me for too long
I talk back to you in my head
Take back the argument we had
Straighten the words
So they'll make sense
Go down smooth, unwrinkled
Taste like the champagne we'd drink
When I paid off my student loans

Conversations always sound better in my head
When I can play you and me
And think about you and me
And the before

I've become a sad dog who chewed up the rug
Hoping you won't make me sleep outside
Yelling at me about a problem we can see
Right here in a heap on the floor

To Go

"Can I get this boxed up?"

I want to take it home for later
Serve myself hot fury for one
At the table with water rings
And a busted leg
That we moved in your truck
From that Craigslist guy last summer

We met on his driveway
The garage behind him
A towering rummage pile
He went on and on about how
The table is an Ethan Allen
And he shouldn't be parting with it
For $50. How stupid.
    Are you going to sell us this table or what?

It's all I can think about
While I sit here with my meal for one

I'm Okay

I walk through the parking lot second guessing if I locked my car door. They're manual locks, so you have to be sure. Decide I did. Pull the front door open and step inside. There's a man behind the counter sporting a black embroidered polo, the gym logo dominantly featured on his chest.

I scan my ID card, stunned from my trance when he asks, "How are you?" with eyes that seem too kind.

I look up directly at him. In a neutral tone, I say, "I'm okay. How about you?"

He draws the words out slowly. He sighs out: "I'm just okay too."

The man and I share a pause. I almost tell him what happened to me at work, and that I'm probably going to hear it from my boss tomorrow.

He breaks the too-long silence: "okay is pretty good for a Thursday."

And now we're back to being strangers. A man behind a desk, and me, checking in.

And so I say, "yes, it's pretty good."

He responds quickly this time, like he's been ready with it: "We're so close"

Of course he meant to the weekend.

I work out, distracted. Let my body take the blow of my day, of the tomorrow in my boss' office. I just keep stacking weight on the barbell. I huff. I puff. I want to blow down this whole damn building.

I have to stop on the way home. Go into Safeway for some medication I need. Turns out it's behind one of those locked cabinets. Still a little sweaty, I walk up to the self-checkout and find an employee. I tell her I need a cabinet open on aisle 10. I made sure to look up before I walked over. She says to go wait and she'll call someone. I walk back over to wait.

The medication I'm waiting for in the locked cabinet is next to the condoms and lube and tampons. Strangely, it's in the same aisle as the Hallmark cards. When people pass by and see me: hair in a frizzy ponytail, and legs busting out of my loud turquoise spandex shorts, I turn to the cards and pretend that I am very carefully choosing one for the perfect occasion.

    When something like 6 minutes pass, I walk back up to tell the employee no one showed. She says it was the wrong aisle number. Then she asks if I needed alcohol or something. I tell her quietly, in the tone we reserve for shame, I need the cabinet unlocked in the feminine health aisle. She laughs and says that's aisle 9. She's laughing at how I got the aisle number wrong. I think.

    She finds the manager that just clocked in. Her name is Grace. She starts following me down the aisle and asks if I needed a ladder or something. I use the tone again. Tell her I need help in the *feminine health* aisle. She goes to retrieve the keys. I'm back in front of this locked glass cabinet next to the retirement and new baby cards I've all but memorized.

    She unlocks the cabinet and I grab my item as stealthily as I can, considering it's a giant purple box. Grace locks the cabinet again and asks for the box. She tells me she'll walk me up to the self-checkout.

    We're walking a few paces before she breaks the silence.

    "You know, I'd let you hold the box," Grace starts. "Not like I don't trust you," she adds. "But I got in trouble last time."

    I nod. I tell her I got in trouble today, too. We're almost at the end of the aisle. I tell her how I made the wrong call at work, and all of the specifics of it. About how and why I'm in trouble. How tomorrow will be with my boss.

    Now we're at the self-checkout stand. All she says is, "wow." Not because it's all that remarkable probably. Maybe she's shocked I told her so much in forty seconds. I told her everything.

Eye of The Storm

When the storm comes
I dig my heels into
The helpless floorboards
Being pried up from their nails,
Wrenching against the sheer force

They give way
And so does my body
Propelled into the eye of your hurricane
My bones brittle
Creak in protest
Seem to whisper, "I told you so"

Even when my limbs tear from their sockets
When my poor ragdoll body
Hits Earth again
Every bone shattered
Into a mosaic of misgivings
I do not wish to unlive
Any second of any moment with you,

I pick up my fragments
Glue them back together
Somehow see it poetic
The way I let myself love
A storm sincere

I'll leave behind a small shard of me for you
So you can remember what it's like
To be loved

It Didn't Hurt Until It Did or Don't Ask Questions You Don't Want The Answer To

If I could live here
In this untruth
A little longer—
That's all I ask

Recipe To Mend A Broken Heart

For best results: before baking, take your wallowing self-pity to sit out for at least a week. Warm to room temperature. Also, make certain your tears don't wet the dry ingredients!

Ingredients:
- 1 cup of obsessive reflection
- ½ cup of resisting the urge to text him
- Several heaping tablespoons of unhealthy habits*
- 1 leveled cup late night phone calls with best friend

Optional Toppings:
- ¾ cup "what-if" statements
- 4 tablespoons denial
- ½ cup of avoiding mutual friends
- 2 tablespoons of sprinkled distractions

Directions:
1. Combine ingredients in a small bowl
2. Start beating the ingredients firmly. Really grind it down.
3. If it's starting to overflow from the bowl or become unmanageable, you're doing it right!
4. Using a rubber spatula, fill an 8X8 pan. Swirl in some of the optional toppings.
5. Bake for 35 minutes at 375°F. Don't let it burn!
6. Let cool before cutting and oversharing with your roommates

Enjoy!

Notes:
*Unhealthy habits: when I made this I used forgetting to eat, lack of sleep, suicidal thoughts, or laying in bed for hours at a time. Adjust to preference.

Part III

Don't Feel Bad At All

I'm polite
I laugh at their jokes
They always pay

They tell me about their tech job
Their dog, sports team, or car
Stand-ins for a personality

I'm distracted by everything
The better conversation at the next table
The tropical drink with a small umbrella on a waiter's tray
I wonder what I would be doing at home if I were alone

I leave the table to check my phone in the bathroom
I'm too civilized to stare at my screen at the table

Order my ride early from inside the stall
I don't owe these men from the internet all of me

They try to make vague future plans
Filled with "after work"s and "see you soon"s

Finish the food they bought me or
Flag down a waiter for a to-go box

I slip into my Uber and out of their life
I *do* have the decency to send a half broken apology
If all goes well, I never hear from them again

I peel away the gossamer curtain from my bedroom window
Let the dimming daylight trace my shadow
Give my body a full up and down check out in the looking glass

Bite my lip into a wry smile and muss my hair just right
Run my palms down my ribs to my waist to my hips
See a me I haven't caught in a while
And don't feel bad at all

(Why Unsending DMs Is A God Send In Your) Hoe Phase

I.
We're lying in bed
        I wouldn't ever call it making love— what we do
You tell me about how a man caught his wife cheating on him
With their linked Fitbits
Her heart rate randomly spiked at 2 am when she was "at a friend's house"
It's funny because I wear a Fitbit
So of course, we have to check my heart rate now

II.
It's the Saturday before Christmas
My friends are hosting a party downtown at this little corner
Dive, Mac's Club
A crumbling brick building packed wall to wall
A plastered gay guy buys me a drink
It's the best
Because he didn't expect anything

I hate going to parties alone
The whole week, I couldn't decide who to invite
Do I invite you?
        We have been *talking* for 3 months
        Used to think I'd make you my boyfriend
But you're flakey
And I got back on the dating apps recently
Having side guys to my side guy

Do I invite him?
        Ocean boy is new
        He's got friends in town from Hawaii
        Says he'll "try to stop by"

My friend Andrew is DJing on the back patio
The theme is Naughty or Nice
My girl Ashley is in a velvet Santa get-up not unlike *Mean Girls*
With a hat jauntily tossed to the side of her bouncy curls

I'm in burgundy tights, a skin tight black skirt, and a see through
shirt embroidered with roses
We sway and swirl to the beat all night

Ashley apparently has the hookup
We keep going behind the bar to pour tequila directly into our
throats
I try to keep the texts from both of my side guys straight
Ocean boy never shows up, and I never invited you

Drunk off too much free liquor now
I wander to the bathroom
A woman who's been eyeing me all night asks to buy me a drink
Now I finally get it

Trying to tell when a woman likes me always seems hard
Her name is Magdalena
She says the girl she's with is *just a friend*
We exchange numbers
I decline the drink because I'm about to leave
Ocean boy's texted me
Made some promises about what he'd do to me
I have to be sober enough to take this Uber

I weave back over to Ashley
Tell her I've got a dick appointment
She squeals
Take a shot for the road
For courage or something
Shit
Forgot I was supposed to stop drinking

III.
His walls are thin
Hometown friends sleeping in the living room
And so we are quiet

I ask him to go down on me
He says no because I must've been sweating

From all that dancing
I still let him love me the wrong way

After, we lay in his bed both perspiring and spooning
I'm annoyed that he's fine touching my sweaty body now
I purse my lips to keep quiet
He groans for me to flick off the lights

My hand searches the floor for my burgundy tights instead
    I don't have to travel far seeing as his mattress is on the ground
He has books. So many books. And posters about fish in Hawaii.
    I always say "never fuck anyone that doesn't have good books"
Bunch up my tights in my hand
Slide one foot in, and slink them up my leg
    There's nothing graceful about putting on tights
    While trying to hastily exit a man's bed

He's shocked I don't want to stay
It's nearly 3 am
I pull my clothes on quickly
Spot a paperback with red pages on the floor
And slip it in my bag

In the Uber home I read a text from Magdalena
I delete it

IV.
I see you on Sunday
Your bed, an immaculate king size
Big enough for you at 6 foot something
Our limbs wrapped up together and quaking
I don't sleep over
You didn't ask me to

V.
On Monday, I workout
I look at my Fitbit log

Apparently on Saturday night I went for a brisk outdoor bike ride
for 15 minutes
I take a screenshot and circle Saturday night in red
I almost text it to you but decide a DM is more lowkey
I hit send
I can't wait to laugh about our "bike ride" with you

I'm looking through Ashley's pictures from Saturday night
Damn, we looked so cute

Shit.
Saturday.
I was with…OCEAN BOY.

Wide-eyed and panicked
I go back to the DM
It doesn't say "seen" yet
I scour the internet for an answer
How do I scrub my shame?!

Go back to the DM
Press and hold until a little dialogue box pops up
"Copy Text" or "Unsend"
UNSEND.
UNSEND.
DEAR GOD.

VI.
The next time we have sex
      I wouldn't ever call it making love— what we do
You ask me to check my Fitbit
My heart rate got up to 153: cardio level
And sure as hell, I was on a midnight bike ride again

FLAMING DOG SHIT

I have a 3 date rule now
I see a future with you
The kind of person that isn't too watery or slow to speak
Or I don't
And I send you *the text*

Feels like all I do is bring bad news
A brown paper bag of dog shit on your porch in flames
You already know what's in there

I watch all the reality TV love shows
Name it. I've seen it.
90 Day Fiancé, Love is Blind, Too Hot to Handle, Married at First Sight, Love Island UK
Never The Bachelor. I don't have cable.

I eat popcorn by the handful and laugh at the stupid couples
Grab my phone and click over to the dating app
I imagine when I find someone, I'll just *know*

When I was young, I was sure I'd be married by now
I've had a few serious relationships
More recently, only situationships
Men I couldn't get to either commit or cast me back into the sea

Soul mates don't exist
You find someone that shovels out a bit of your lonely
Laughs at the right times
Makes you feel seen
That, I believe

And when they hit the 3rd date and the sky hasn't opened up
Mufasa hasn't given me a great big pep talk about this being my destiny
When it feels so ordinary
I leave another bag of flaming dog shit on his porch

I wonder when it'll be my turn

Someday, I'll open my door
Stomp out the flames, my foot squelching in molten feces
And know that I deserve this

I Should "Allow" Men To Date Me

You said, "should be home by 7"
I wore my nice underwear
Black, see through, stitched in delicate roses
My bra a lacy number,
X straps exposing my back, nipples mostly visible
Not quite a set
Never thought I had an occasion for lingerie
Or that any man deserved it

All dressed up and nowhere to go
I wait on my couch for hours
Decide I'm done giving the benefit of the doubt
I slide into my bedroom
Strip down and look myself up and down in the full length mirror
In just my *almost matching* black lace
Not ready to take it off yet

I finally wipe my face
I put on winged eyeliner for this?
Lie down, drifting, as my bed melts into my skin

My phone buzzes
"Hey whatsup?"

I make you wait a few minutes
Shake my head at how quickly I jump for you
You ask me to come over
I mock you, "Is it booty call o'clock?"
You say you feel bad and that I don't have to come
I stop giving you a hard time because you owe me an evening

I don't leave the house 'til 11:30
Still mad I already took off my makeup

Your television glows and murmurs in the background
We slide between your sheets
Our clothes coming off in pieces

Your fingers run hungrily over my body
Find my delicate lacy bra and underwear
You call them "pretty"
I say "I know" instead of with a softer "thanks"
You don't notice they don't quite match
And I don't want to slow down and talk
I'm here to collect what's mine
So I let you think I have a pretty lingerie set

I tell you what to do
And don't let you get any pleasure first
My thighs tighten around your head
Holding you in just the right spot
I see my mismatched black lace on the floor
That pretended to belong together all night

My back arches and my hips slide lower toward you
My eyes close and I cover my gasping mouth
In that moment, I decide from now on
I should "allow" men to date me

Rattled

You were a shitty boyfriend, but I didn't *really* know that. We were at a Lazy Dog chain restaurant and you gave me a purple-bluish stone, some silver earrings, and a navy TAHOE sweater.

My head whipped back, forehead creased, and eyebrows raised in surprise: "Earrings, wow. They're so pretty."

You chuckled, "Is this the first time I've given you jewelry in our two years together?" We shrugged, looked left to right and at each other, drew a blank and decided that yes, it was the first time.

"How was your trip?" I pined.

You told me about it. Mostly about some girl who was relentlessly trying to hook up with you. A few months ago, you convinced me to make our relationship open. Or poly. But you hated that word.

"It's not poly," you'd say, "poly is whack. It's *open*" Whatever. I hated both words and the whole thing. But you bragged about this dumb girl who wanted to bang you and then gave me this bruised stone.

When we said goodbye in the parking lot you stuck your entire hand down the back of my pants. My butt wiggled, a worm dancing out of your claws.

"Why are you such a prude? No one can see us" you grinned. I yanked your hand into the daylight, squeamishly hugged and pecked you until next time.

Chhhhh dunk chhhhh dunk chhhh dunk. The stone rattles in the cubby handle of my car door. I kept the stone after I gave you up. Let it rattle in my car door for months. It haunted and comforted me. Every time I closed the door of my Nissan, it was there.

I started dissociating at work. For a minute or two, I'd be convinced life wasn't real and I wasn't me. This body felt foreign. I signed up for therapy at Kaiser. Went to one awkward appointment.

The therapist and I exchanged names. I told her why I was there. She told me things I didn't want to hear. I cried.

I didn't tell her I thought I wasn't me sometimes. Or that I didn't want to be here. 30 minutes dinged. I left.

I lost 15lbs on the depression diet. Let that dumb little stone rattle me.

My hands on the steering wheel. The stereo tuned to '98.1 The Breeze' with Delilah's velvety embrace wafting through the dying light. Heard the chhhh dunk settle at the stoplight. I fingered the stone, turned its grooves around in my hand. A rock you'd skip on a waveless lake. Glanced up at the stoplight– still red. I cranked the manual window all the way down as Delilah dedicated *Hold On Loosely* to a lonely caller. I rested my arm out the door, let my hand spread eagle.

Plunk.

Green light.

God Bless

After William Ward Butler and Sam Sax

> God bless my mother & the vodka that loves her & God bless my father & the words he will never say. God bless my brother turned sister turned sibling & the transition. God bless the one I pushed away & the woman who came out for her. God bless the stone I let settle. God bless my parents & my life I hid from them & God bless my sibling who came out when I couldn't. God bless my mother & her speeches from The Bible. God bless my lost faith. God bless my modern praise without a name.

Balloons

A month after,
I was walking a few streets from my house
I looked up
Saw 3 balloons tied together
Fighting each other high in the cloudless sky

I felt vaguely sorry

Reminded of you & when we went flying
Two person plane at night over the Bay Area lights

The balloons tug-o-warred each other
Racing to be the first to the blue open
I tried to summon a sadness from my gut
Some pang of remembering you

The sun in my eyes
Hand over my brow
I kept staring, squinting, blinking
Watching those 3 balloons get smaller,
And higher

Photo Gallery

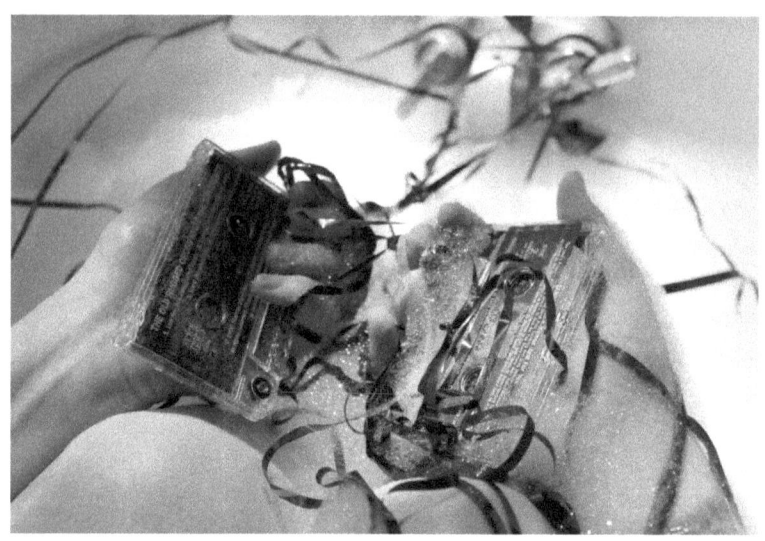

Thank You

A special, heartfelt thank you to the following individuals and collectives who understood and supported the vision of this book:

Edgar Gallegos, your graphic design and photography skills made the visuals come to life. You translated the images from my brain beautifully.

Katelyn Yarnold, you offered your home and clawfoot bathtub to help me achieve these photos. You also dragged that 250 lbs bathtub up a hill with us for the perfect shot. That's a friend.

The Unnameables, formerly known as "Writers Group," Emer Martin, Cory Massaro, Ruben Zamora, David Perez, Mighty Mike McGee, and other members who have joined us over the years, thank you for reading, critiquing, and re-reading these pieces. Our close-reads, discussions, and banter have sustained me in every way. I appreciate your dedication and friendship.

Rawmeash, the artist led, independent publishing co-operative, you gave my book a place to live in the ether. You believed in the power of my work.

Kinetic Poetics Project of UC Santa Cruz, you were my first real stage and community of artists. If I had never seen your flyer at a bus stop in 2011 and come to a poetry slam, my writing would have lived in my notebook forever. And probably always rhymed.

Acknowledgements

These pieces have appeared in the following collections prior to this publication:

Two Minutes (Caesura, 2023)

God Bless (Porter Gulch Review, 2022)

About The Author

Jacqueline Gallegos, known as Jacqnasty on the stage, is from the Bay Area, California. She now lives on the California Central Coast with her family. She has never moved away from the Golden State, but travels anytime she has a buck, a calling, and a few days off.

She was a member of the Santa Cruz Legendary Poetry Slam Team, placing 8th in the nation at The National Poetry Slam. Her work has appeared in *Red Wheelbarrow*, *Chinquapin*, *Porter Gulch Review*, and *Caesura*. Her first book *Not Yet Fluent in Luminescence* was published by Space Cadet Records in 2015.